CONTENT

JANUARY 2014 – IS IT A GOOD START

I mean well, but ....

FEBRUARY 2014 – WILL I EVER BE SLIM FOR MY HOLIDAY?

Well, I can always dream

MARCH 2014 – I WILL NEVER GIVE UP ... YET!

Arrows can go down as well as up!

APRIL 2014 – GEORGE ARRIVES

A not so friendly alien

MAY – I MAY OR MAY NOT …….

I'm a trier if nothing else

JUNE AND JULY 2014 – MADEIRA WAS LOVELY

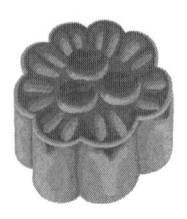

But so was the cake …………..

AUGUST AND SEPTEMBER 2014 – NO MORE WINE FOR ME

Two glasses and both empty!

OCTOBER AND NOVEMBER 2014 – THE DIET HAS COME TO AN END

For the time being anyway

4 January 2014

Today was the start of a positive year
As to Jump Start class I went
Rachel and Steph were up on the stage
And positive vibes they sent
There were many of us who were down on the floor
Shaking out bits and bobs
My sister and I were doing our best
In fact we did a very good job
For about 90 minutes we exercised
And we all had a laugh as well
I'm looking forward to classes this year
My enthusiasm you could tell
I asked to be weighed before the start
As I hadn't been for some time
I jumped on the scales with baited breath
And waited for the sign
But blow me down (I don't like to swear)
I'd dropped by a pound and a half
I was quite shocked and very surprised
and said "are you having a laugh?"
But no, the scales were telling the truth
Which made me feel even better
So two classes a week I will attend
And lose weight and be a go-getter.

19 January

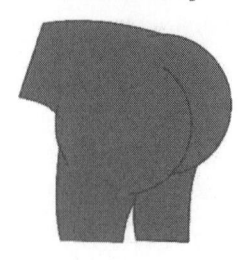

A couple of weeks has passed me by
And to my friends I will not lie
It's only half a pound I've lost
And quite a few bob it's actually cost
But I could easily have put it on
So I'm doing right and not doing wrong
But I'm back on steroids to help me get better
And I stick to the diet to the very letter
'Cause if I don't, I know weight I will gain
It happened before, I was entirely to blame
But my Fat Club girls' holiday is approaching fast
And a few more pounds must be removed from my arse

20 February

Apologies to all my friends
This illness seems to never end
And then my old computer crashed
And I lost my work, it all got mashed
But now I am writing my verses once more
I'm still on the steroids and I weigh slightly more
But I won't give up and I won't despair
I can still paint my nails and style my hair
I went to class this very night
And my trackie bottoms felt a little tight
But I jumped about and twisted and turned
So hundreds of calories I must have burned
I have lots of appointments with the NHS
But they are looking after me, though I may look a mess
I know the weight has not been lost
But I must get healthy, so I don't give a toss
But then again, that isn't true
Cause when I'm fat I'm feeling blue
But I'm off to Portugal a week tomorrow
So no time for tears, or fears or sorrow
The bikini might not come out this time
But I won't let it stop me from trying the wine

22 February

Today I bought a suitcase
In readiness for my hols
I'm getting quite excited
And looking forward to seeing the girls
I've tried on some of my 'summer' clothes
(As I'm hoping it will be hot)
And believe it or not they still fit me
And my cozzie still fits round my bot!
I'm gonna try and exercise
And do my very best
And also to sit down by the pool
Where I will be able to have a rest
I'm spending time with my sister
And I'm sure we'll have some fun
We'll enjoy the wine and have a dance
And maybe lose inches off our bum

24 February

Today it is a Sunday

And it started pretty good

But as the day went further along

I stopped doing as I should

A chocolate cake and a packet of crisps

I couldn't help myself

And the dreaded choccy praline bar

That I'd hidden on the shelf

Three vodkas downed when at the pub

With an added diet coke

Then off to the Brit for food and wine

Then home for a bit of a poke!

By poke I mean on Facebook

As my friends had done the same

I really should do some exercise

And not play these silly games

But a visit to see the family

Had me dancing all about

My grandson got the Wii out

I was knackered, and that's no doubt

But I felt quite good and confident

That I could beat him once or twice

But as I'm over 58

To win often would not be nice

But this all happened before the wine

And before my scampi and chips

This Sunday really hasn't been good

And it's all ended up on my hips!

26 February

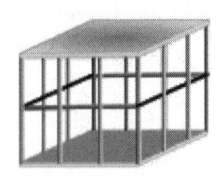

A long and tiring day at work
I'm really feeling my age
And the amount I eat and drink all day
I should be locked up in a cage
I just can't get the balance right
'tween healthy food and bad
An apple, a pear or a bar of choc
OMG it's sending me mad
The steroids I'm taking could be to blame
As they make me want to eat
But I'll keep on trying the best I can
I will not admit defeat

27 February

Some of the girls are over there
Propping up the bar
I plan on meeting them all tomorrow
And you know who you are!
Be ready with a glass of wine
That's exactly what I will need
But don't be drunk before we meet
My warnings you should heed
Cause although I plan on having a drink
Whilst I'm waiting for the plane
I promise to behave myself
Yeh, alright, I know – INSANE!

28 February

Sat at the airport waiting to fly
A big glass of wine, oh my, oh my
Might have another whilst I wait for my flight
Shall I wrestle with conscience? not much of a fight
Soon be in Faro, then off to hotel
More glasses of wine to be had, who can tell?

28 February

Now I'm sat on the plane
There's a space next to me
So I've plenty of room
Oh joy, oh glee
Drinks coming round
Plus a chicken salad wrap
But nothing for me
Ooh wait, what's that?
Vodka and diet, I think I might
See, conscience again
And not much of a fight

28 February

The drinks trolley came round, as I mentioned before
The vodka has gone, and I'd really like more
But I must not misbehave, or my sis will disown
Mind you, she's not here and I am all alone
And they may not come back and offer another
Shall I or not? no I cannot be bothered
Tonight I will drink and dance and have fun
And start the campaign to lose weight off this bum

28 February

Had a good night of dancing and fun
And I twerked some calories off me bum
The jugs of Sangria came thick and fast
And after 'a few!' I thought "will I last?"
But I did and eventually left about two
Fulfilled and happy and tiddly too

1 March

Up at dawn for breakfast
Couldn't resist the cake
Scrambled eggs and beans
How much more can my stomach take?
As I stood myself next to the toaster
Losing the will to live
I thought to myself – as I often do
"Will the zip on me trousers give?
But no it stayed (as it is re-enforced)
Alright, that may not be true
But after 3-days of food and booze
I may gain a pound or two

1 March

At 11am I got ready
For my treatment of the day
A hand and foot massage I had
And my troubles just melted away
The treatment room was relaxing
And the smell it was devine
I felt relaxed and slightly dozy
But friends say I'm like that all the time

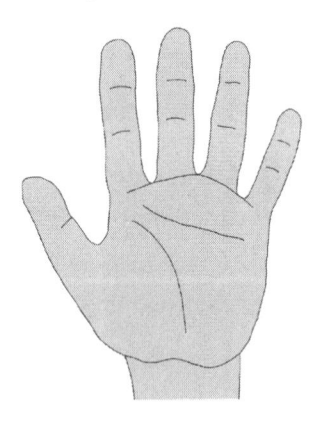

1 March

We all walked into Alvor
Well what a walk that was
The rain came down and the wind did blow
WE SHOULD HAVE CAUGHT THE BUS!!
We finally arrived at the restaurant
But the only seats were outside
So we all sat down and shivered
And embarrassed, we had to decide
Should we stay and be cold or up and leave?
We decided on the latter
So back into the wind and rain
To find us somewhere better
We didn't go far, just across the road
Where we settled down in the warm
Lots of food and drink and good company
And safe from the awful storm
Again we hit the Sangria
And plenty of jugs were had
Our five a day were plentiful
But were we really being bad?
The girls all chose from the menu
And fish was the meal of the day
But me, I had an omelette
Yes, boring, I know, but hey!

1 March

After a shower and making ourselves up
Dinner was on our mind
What calorie free meals were on offer tonight?
It didn't matter, we'd eat what we'd find
Again the drinks came thick and fast
And we all indulged in a few
Well it was our Anna's birthday
And it would have been very rude not to

2 March

Up with the larks and feeling refreshed
To the restaurant I did go
It was breakfast time and I needed to eat
So I had melon and yoghurt - and oh!
Look at the cake just sitting there
It's definitely looking at me
Oh bugger, it's calling me over
And I pick it up with glee
Back to my table I do go
Feeling happy, but guilty as well
But I'm all on my own, so no-one will see
And there's only me who can tell

2 March

Today at 11 I'm having a treat
An hour of being spoiled
I'm really looking forward to it
And the smell of the lovely oils
As I was waiting patiently
Laura came into the room
"I'm your therapist, welcome" she said
"You'll be feeling relaxed real soon"
I had a wonderful back massage
And was really very surprised
As Laura had the strongest hands
For someone of such a small size
She exfoliated first and massaged my legs
I felt as though I were in heaven
And you would never have thought she was on her own
As she had the strength of seven
(Thank you Laura)

2 March

Sunday night was very quiet
As some were leaving early
But we all still managed a drink or two
And it's fun being with the girlies
Our Fat Club weekend has been a success
And we are looking forward to June
So again starts the job of losing some weight
And getting my body back in tune

3 March

A lot of girls have now gone home
So I'm sitting and writing my verse
I've not really spent all that much
As there's money still in my purse
So today I had a treatment
Reflexology, and boy was it good
She removed the stresses and strains of life
Which I didn't think she could
Now I'm just about to have a drink
Hot chocolate and Baileys, it is
A lot of calories and not good for you
But it's way too early for fizz

3 March

It was 2pm when we left the hotel
As we had to catch our flight
At least I wasn't travelling alone
There were three others on my flight
Before I left I had some lunch
A cheese toastie and some chips
With a very large glass of Matheus
And all three will end up on my hips
I'm now on the plane in row 15F
And I've just had a vodka and coke
My mobile is also on flight mode time
So on Facebook I cannot poke
I've met some lovely ladies this time
And we've all had a lot of fun
But now the hard work really begins
To remove this fat from around me bum

Love My Leisure

The girls from Love My Leisure
Have really done us proud
Our leaders are the best of the best
They really stand out in a crowd
They organise us with strict precision
And everything goes to plan
We all have a laugh and exercise too
See, to have fun, we don't need a man!
The treatments have been amazing
And Trudy has taken charge
Us girlies are from all walks of life
Some tiny, some little, some (me) large
But it doesn't matter to any of us
As we are all in the very same boat
Weight needs to be lost and exercise done
Love My Leisure will keep us afloat

Love My Leisure

3 March

It's half past 6 in the evening
And the plane is running late
The awful wind is against us
(and I don't mean from what we ate!)
Our arrival time has been delayed
By about 30 minutes or more
But it can't be helped, it's no-ones fault
So I won't moan and be a bore
Hubby will be waiting for me
As I step through the arrival gate
I'm sure he won't be that distressed
If I am a few minutes late
I've still not eaten since 1pm
So my willpower is pretty strong
But someone's just reminded me
Of a chocolate muffin, how wrong!
But I didn't eat every bit of it
I left a few of the crumbs
But it hasn't done me very much harm
As I'm sat down and you can't see me bum

9 March

It's Sunday lovely Sunday
And the sun is shining too
I've been to the pub and had a few wines
Well what else should a girlie do?
I've just come home and I need to eat
But we're having dinner later on
A sandwich and diet coke for now
Surely that is not so wrong?
But actually I'm feeling tiddled
So I'm glad that dinner is prepared
Hubby is happy to wait till 8
And I must say I think that's fair
But the calories that I have consumed
In a bottle of wine alone
Has probably left me with none for food
Quick Samaritans, give me the phone!
But it really doesn't bother me
As life is really too short
As health and happiness is top of my list
And if I'm crafty, I'll never get caught!

12 March

It's not very often I feel like this
But today I'm feeling blue
My health has taken another bad turn
And I'm struggling to know what to do
This isn't a verse that I usually write
And I don't plan on it happening again
I'm feeling fat, I'm looking fat
I want to be different, but when?
Be positive I tell everyone else
And keep that smile on your face
And if you see me in the street
Please give me a wee bit of space
In a couple of days my smile will be back
And I'll be laughing and joking about
So please don't think that I've lost my touch
I'll be back, and of that there's no doubt

17 March - St Patricks Day

Any excuse to celebrate
With wine in my glass and some food on my plate
But I'm sitting at home, not feeling quite right
And I think it's because my waistband's too tight
The muffin top has spread wider and wider
And if I wore a tent, it still wouldn't hide her!
The mirror has stopped telling me all of those lies
And all it says now is "YOU ate all the pies"
It is only me who can sort this all out
There'll be no more excuses, of that there's no doubt

22 March

For the last few days, I've been very good
As my doctor told me I must
My plan is to rid me of 28 pounds
From all areas except my bust
I have realised just how much I eat
And how much of it is so bad
So it's no more crisps or praline bars
Or the muffins that I had
I sat down to think about what I ate
In just one ordinary day
And the calories really mounted up
And I really don't know what to say
So Fitness Pal is being used
And I am being 99% good
I allow myself a little treat
As I think that everyone should
So wish me luck as I start, yet again
On this journey to be much lighter
I am writing all my calories down
I'm nothing if not a fat fighter

1 April

Today is April Fool's Day
And I'm sure I'm the butt of the joke
As my tummy wobbles and boobies droop
Only on Facebook do I get a poke!
I've not been well. Again? you say
But I really do try my best
I eat healthily and exercise
In my trackies and posh string vest
But the vest is getting tighter
And the holes are expanding fast
And the way my belly's bulging
I don't think it's gonna last
The fat will poke through every hole
And those holes will start to stretch
How I wish I was back in my leotard
When the young men used to letch!

12 April

It's been over a week since I last wrote a verse

And my diet's no better, in fact it's got worse

Chocolate muffins and crisps and those dam praline bars

Have seen the pounds pile on, especially my arse

Yet again I've been poorly, and I should lose some weight

But to be portly and podgy, it must be my fate

In my dreams I am lovely and sexy and slim

And I'm 5ft 10 with legs up to my chin

But reality arrives when I wake from my sleep

And I stand at the mirror and take a quick peep

Well the legs have shrunk and I'm 5ft 2

My waist's disappeared, where's it gone? Not a clue

And the muffin top's spreading wider and wider

And it's all down to this crap I'm putting inside her

But summer is coming and I've nothing to wear

So I must start being strict and must really take care

I can't live in a dream for the rest of my days

As my being fat isn't only a phase

I must get a grip and sort myself out

I'll still be 5ft 2, but perhaps not as stout

24 April

Again I disappeared from view
But not in the way I'd like me to!
Been working hard but feeling grim
It's bloody hard work to get me slim
My tummy is bloated and I'm looking so round
But there's something not right, says the ultra sound
My poor old liver and gall bladder too
Have a bit of a problem, not sure what to do
Seeing the doctor in the next few days
And I bet I have to give up my wicked ways
There's also an alien called George, in my tum
Who keeps moving about when I'm sat on me bum
I know it sounds mad but he's definitely there
And he causes me pain, so George beware
I know you love food and don't like the wine
So if I can stop eating, then all will be fine!

5 May

A lot of tests and not so much food

Not stopped the wine, as that would be rude

No gall stones so that is one result

But liver enlarged, of that there's no doubt

I'm trying to cut down on all fatty foods

But it's getting real hard and causes bad moods

I just really wish that I could be well

Cause I'm feeling real crap, but most days you can't tell

But enough of these negative thoughts and tales

I'm gonna lose weight and I WILL NOT FAIL!!!

22 May

It's getting harder every day

I'm struggling, I'm ashamed to say

I've cut out all the crisps and bread

The chocolate's gone, to me it's dead!

I have salad for lunch and a yoghurt too

Special K for breakfast, so what more can I do?

My dinner isn't very big and sometimes I have none

But all this dieting and going without has no effect on me bum

I cannot do the exercise as I've hurt my flaming knee

And both my feet are swollen, Oh woe is bloody me

Blood test on my liver is happening tomorrow

I think I'll hand my body parts back and from an athlete I'll borrow

New legs, new knees, and a body that's fit

And if that doesn't work, then b***** and s***!!!!

4 June – Our trip to Madeira

Off to the airport we both did go
My sister Jan and I
We were off on our hols with the Fat Club girls
And soon we were in the sky
We were very restrained and we did behave
And no drink was had on the plane
But two bottles of sparkling wine at the bar
Should really have put us to shame

Later on
We all arrived at the Pestana Grand
And what a hotel it was
5 stars with all the extras as well
And they laid on a courtesy bus!
Now why, do you ask, do I mention the bus?
Well I noticed it was rather hilly
And lagging behind people older than me
Well, I thought it might make me look silly

5 June

I was up at 8 and wanted to eat

So to the restaurant I did go

A glass of Bucks Fizz and some waffles too

And some chocolate croissants, oh no!

These few days of fitness have already stopped

But hey, life is too short

So I'll enjoy the wine, the food and more

And hope I don't get caught

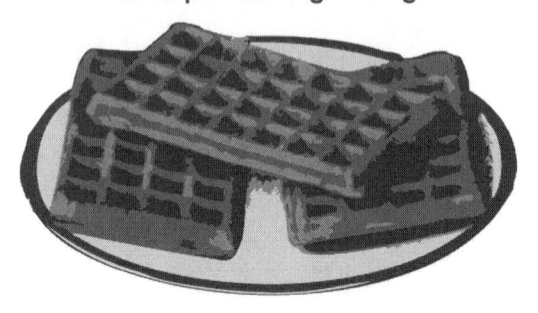

5 June

Today we went down to Funchal town and a lovely place it is

We wandered around, enjoyed the views just me and my little sis

We decided to stop at a little café, where we ordered a couple of drinks

A nice cup of coffee was ordered for Jan but I sat and I had a think

One of my favourite wines I saw it was Matheus Rose of course

So half a bottle I thought I'd have (you know me, I can't keep of the sauce)

After the drinks we were heading back and were accosted by a very nice man

"You like a ride in my Tuk Tuk" he said, to get back t'hotel was the plan

Well Jan and I decided to go and we gave him 5 Euros each

He took us the scenic route as well, well isn't life a peach?

Our hair blew about, we bumped up and down we were given a guided tour

Mauricio was our driver's name and he was a lifeguard too – phwor

We eventually got back to the hotel and got changed and sat round the pool

The sun was hot and we just relaxed and ordered Kia Royals – we're no fools

We noticed a couple of pleasant sights blue shorts, great legs, nice bum

But we managed to restrain ourselves (well we weren't out here to have fun!)

That same night

In the evening we all got dressed up to the nines
And down to the bar we went
A few more drinks were had by all
And our dance moves we thought we should vent
A man on guitar who sang us some songs
Eventually got into his groove
And us girls, once we managed to get off our chairs
Decided to show him some moves

6 June

The aerobics class was a bit of a scream
If they made me do that, I'd think they were mean
Jumping and stretching and bobbing about
Arm came too close, oops, gave her a clout
Teacher was fit and spoke Portuguese
God, I'll never do that, not with these knees
One lovely man amongst all of the girls
With their hats and bikinis, costumes and curls
He kept afloat and did all he could
But I bet that tomorrow, he will feel like wood
Fair play to them all as I'm sat on the side
Just watching and enjoying and trying to hide

Lorraine's Birthday

Well what can I say about Lorraine?

Whose birthday it is today

I've only known her a couple of years

But she's lovely in every way

When we're at our classes and we stand at the back

Lorraine certainly gives it her all

She sings along to all the songs

And her arms are a free for all

She throws herself into every routine

And I can honestly say

That without Lorraine in our great little group

There'd be no-one to get in the way!

Happy Birthday Lorraine

6 June

Today I had my treatment

It was going to take an hour

My back and my legs were massaged well

And then I took a shower

But silly me had been out in the sun

Just a couple of hours before

And I didn't realise my back had burnt

And I can honestly say I swore

But being a brave little Fat Club member

I braved it through the pain

Only to go back to the pool

Where it was pouring down with rain

6 June

This evening we all dressed up to the nines
And headed down to eat
and as I struggled down the stairs
I noticed my swollen feet
And then I noticed the rest of me
And thought "that's swollen too"
But it's not the food and drink I've had
Surely not, that can't be true

7 June

As up at 7 and showered and dressed
But my suntan marks looked a bit of a mess
I'll cover them up until they calm down
Eventually they'll turn a nice shade of brown
Went down to breakfast for waffles/Bucks Fizz
Should I have something else, oh my mind's in a tizz
Food hasn't been banned, nor wine come to that
And I am on holiday and I'm not really fat
At the moment I'm sitting outside in the cold
With a towel round my shoulders, well I wouldn't be told
The sun is still rising and will be here real soon
But if that doesn't happen, I'm off back to me room

7 June

A wonderful day was had by all
We laid in the sun around the pool
Bikinis and cossies were all on show
And we all looked fabulous, don't you know
Our healthy eating had gone to plan
As chocolates and crisps we all did ban
I know some will believe that it isn't true
But we only tell white lies, as girls often do

7 June

It was happy hour down at the bar
And we gathered in our hoards
Different drinks for different girls
So no chance of being bored
The service was a bit of a joke
And we waited for what seemed an age
But my little sister took charge of things
And at the waiter she did rage
After a lot of tooing and froing
We finally got our drinks
And the first two rounds we got for free
So it pays to kick up a stink

7 June

After dinner a few girls got together
To watch the fireworks in the town
A group of us headed for the posh hotel
And cocktails we did down
The fireworks started at half past ten
And we watched from the balcony
A "Banging Crescendo" and some "Fizzy Bobblers"
Were what we were waiting to see
Our evening didn't disappoint
And we slowly walked back home
And when we finally reached the hotel
Straight to bed to rest weary bones

8 June

It's our last full day in Madeira
And the sun is yet again hot
We've had our breakfast and a glass of Bucks Fizz
And we're all round the pool like a shot
I know it's only 10 o'clock
But it never is too early
To strip off our clothes and lay in the sun
With all the lovely girlies

Well most of the day was spent by the pool
And the tans are coming on great
Some are red, some are brown and a few are pink
And some of us look a right state
We've been real good and not stuffed our faces
And I have even lost weight
No chocolate or crisps have been hanging around
But it's at home that that's where they'll wait

Goodbye Madeira

Our very last night in Madeira
And we all dressed up so posh
My black and white dress got an airing
And we all went down for some nosh
As usual I ate my salad
Then the chicken and veg went down well
And the pud tonight was to die for
There's an inch on my waist, I can tell
After our meal we went to the bar
Where a singer was doing his bit
In fact he had a pretty good voice
So we decided to stay and sit
But then it all got too much for us
And the dance floor beckoned us on
We bopped, we twisted, we wiggled about
And the inch on my waist has gone

9 June – going home

Up quite early for breakfast
And I sat outside to eat
We have to leave at 10 am
So no time for anymore treats
But I forgot to mention that yesterday, I had a pedicure
Kate helped me relax as she pampered my feet
And I felt I was dancing on air
The coach will be arriving soon
And we'll be on our way
But a great big thanks to all the girls
Whose company made my day

28 June

It seems I've been away so long
No verses done, no rhyme nor song
I have been busy with my sister Jan
Looking after parents as much as we can
But hopefully Dad will be home real soon
And verses will come with a bang and a boom
But all this work has been worthwhile
As the size of my waistband has made me smile
My white linen trousers, well they kept falling down
So a belt was required when out in the town
No-one else would have noticed this very small change
But my clothes now cover a very wide range
Size 12 and 14 and a sixteen too
And there's a 10 in the back, so I know what to do
Just keep on working and don't stop to eat
Just the odd glass of wine for a special wee treat

29 June

It's Sunday again and it should be a roast
But we have been known to have cheese on toast
Two chocolate muffins that went down a treat
If I eat anymore then I won't see my feet
I really do try and stick to the plan
But it's difficult when you live with a man
Who can eat what he likes without getting fat
And who has second helpings of this, this and that!

5 July

Two chocolate eclairs and a diet coke
And a chocolate muffin as well
Well this old diet isn't going so good
And that you can probably tell
It could be the weather, it could be owt else
But I really should not be so bad
My waistline was doing really well
It had gone down by just a tad
But now my belly is round and robust!
And my trousers I cannot do up
But never fear, I'll get over it
And a wine tonight I will sup!

13 July

So now I've been told that I must not drink
Well, not as much as I did!
It's gonna be hard and I know I might fail
So I'll remove the bottles I hid!
But hey, this might be just the thing
To help in the quest to lose weight
Just think of all of those calories not had
And my body won't look such a state
I am very determined to get myself fit
But I know it will take some time
But I've done it before when I lost 2 stone
And I really did feel mighty fine
My belly went flat and my bum was a peach
And my bingo wings had flown
And I only want to lose a few pounds
I don't want to be skin and bone

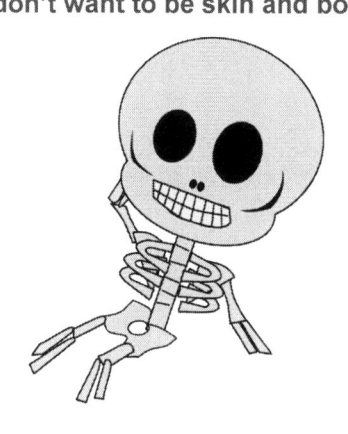

17 July

Well I've finally had to admit defeat
No classes for me for a while
I've not been well for quite some time
But you wouldn't know by my smile
But diet and exercise is now second place
As I must get healthy again
But my verses won't stop, only exercise will
As my body is struggling with pain

24 July

It's really hot and I'm not able to cope
I've tried salads and fruit
But it seems there's no hope
My belly is huge and I look 6 months gone
And as I'm 58, that would really be wrong
The will power's gone and I've just given up
And not even a wine am I able to sup
Fed up with doctors who say 'must lose weight'
To be short fat and round
Is this truly my fate?
I can't even exercise or jump up and down
As it all starts to wobble
Which then makes me frown
I need an incentive, but what can that be?
There's nothing exciting that's happening to me
So I must get myself out of this hole
And be strong and sort myself out
And if anyone sees me stuffing my face
Please, do feel free to shout

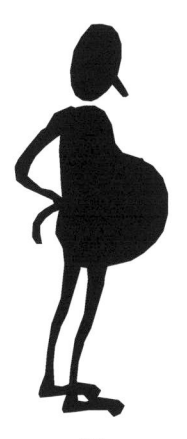

5 August

A little bit of weight I've lost
As no more wine I drink
And it seems that certain foods are bad
As in my tummy, they kick up a stink
I am hoping this is all due to the fact
That I've cut down on most things sweet
And that it isn't due to not being well
I should know within the week

16 August

It's been a while since a Fat Club verse
But as you know, I haven't been well
The diet has really gone to pot
And my stomach has started to swell
But this time not through food alone
And I'm also off the wine
They reckon that if I abstain
Then everything will be fine
So I'm going back to Fat Club
And I'm gonna follow the rules
And abide by what the leader says
It's like being back at school

4 September

See how long I've been away
And apologies to you all
Yet again, I've not been well
And not able to play the fool
I'm having problems eating food
What? Never, I hear you say
But there's something wrong inside my tum
And it just won't go away
Another trip to hospital
Is definitely on the cards
I really wish I knew what it was
As I'm finding it pretty hard
Salads and yoghurts are all I can eat
And even those are not too good
My tummy bloats to twice its size
And feels solid like a piece of wood
I also have an alien that runs around my tum
I've affectionately called him George
And he's the only one having fun
He runs about causing havoc and pain
Until the tablets make him stop
But when he comes back and starts again
I fear my tummy, it may go pop

2 October

A hospital trip is on the cards
As I still am having pains
I lost a bit of weight last week
But this time I think I've gained
It's really hard to get it right
When everything makes you ill
Am living off bits of fruit and ham
And the glasses of wine are NIL
But it's difficult to stay in line
When I'm taking so many pills
And some say, why do I bother?
When I'm always feeling ill
Well if I didn't keep a check
Even on the smallest things
My weight would spiral out of control
And I would end up the size of twins

18 October

Not been to class for a couple of weeks
As feeling pretty rough
I have to go to hospital
And if that is not enough
A camera will investigate
The top half and the bottom
This diet isn't working
And I'm feeling pretty rotten
I lost some weight when it all began
But now I'm back to fat old me
I'm not eating much, but can't exercise
So someone hear my plea
Don't show me where the chocolate is
Or the packets of low fat crisps
Cause they're only low if you eat only one
And not four or five or six!
I will go back to class real soon
And behave in a normal way
And my pills and excuses will have to go
And the 'truth' game I will have to play

My final verse
2 November

I have finally had to succumb
To the roundness of me bum
The diet is now on hold
How many times has that been told?
But it's no good kidding myself
With the choccies and crisps on the shelf
It's had to come to a stop
With a jump and a skip and a hop
And that's my final exercise
But to some it will be no surprise
So farewell to all my friends out there
I wish you well wherever you are
And the next time you will hear from me
My weight I hope will be 9 stone 3

Printed in Great Britain
by Amazon.co.uk, Ltd.,
Marston Gate.